Lady, wilt thou love me?

Eighteen love poems for Ellen Terry attributed to
GEORGE BERNARD SHAW

Edited with introduction and notes by
JACK WERNER

STEIN AND DAY/*Publishers*/New York

First published in the United States of America in 1980
Copyright © 1980 by Jack Werner
Printed in the United States of America
Stein and Day/*Publishers*/Scarborough House
Briarcliff Manor, New York 10510

Library of Congress Cataloging in Publication Data

Shaw, George Bernard, 1856-1950.
    Lady, wilt thou love me?

    1. Shaw, George Bernard, 1856-1950 — Manuscripts —
Facsimiles. 2. Love poetry, English. I. Terry,
Ellen, Dame, 1848-1928. II. Werner, Jack. III. Title.
PR5364.L3   1980   .821'.912   80-20009
ISBN 0-8128-2758-9

Contents

Introduction

As every schoolboy knows, Bernard Shaw is acknowledged to be the greatest dramatist since Shakespeare. Over a quarter of a century since his death, the result of a fall in his garden in 1950 at the ripe old age of 94, his name is still as much a household word as ever it was, and is likely to remain so as long as people are interested in the theatre and literature.

Shaw is recognised as a master of prose. Few know of him as a writer of verse though his output in this field is very considerable, as my researches in the British Museum and other great libraries have proved. Produced mainly in the early part of his career, the verses are chiefly on the subject of love though generally in a tongue-in-cheek flippant vein.

That he could also write serious love poems of an intensely passionate kind, which frequently rise to considerable heights of lyrical beauty and sensitivity of feeling in marked contrast to his general style, is demonstrated in the entrancing set of eighteen love poems addressed to the great actress Ellen Terry, now presented for the first time in this collection.

As in prose, so also in verse Shaw revels in the exuberance of his own verbosity. In the words of the redoubtable Dr Samuel Johnson, in many respects his counterpart of one-and-a-half centuries earlier, Shaw was in his element in 'the enduring elegance of female friendship', which he expressed so vivaciously and eloquently in his remarkable exchange of letters with Ellen Terry begun in the 1890s, a 'paper courtship' which forms one of the most brilliant correspondences in the annals of English letter writing. Shaw also revelled in 'paper courtships' with other members of the opposite sex, notably celebrated actresses.

[4]

453   SHAW (G. B.) SERIES OF 18 AUTOGRAPH MANUSCRIPT LOVE POEMS
TO ELLEN TERRY, *each poem written on one side only of an octavo leaf, un-*
bound, contained in a specially made slipcase, half morocco   8vo

.   UNPUBLISHED. A remarkable and sustained outpouring of pas-
sionate verse, forming a hitherto unknown addition to the celebrated " paper
courtship " of Ellen Terry which produced the brilliant series of letters
between the two. The poems are written in a variety of metres (including
the sonnet form) and vary in length from eight to twenty-four lines: their
passionate seriousness distinguishes them from most of the few other known
love poems by Shaw, which are usually more or less flippant in tone.

In these manuscripts Shaw has attempted to disguise his normal writing,
employing for example a number of unnatural loops and flourishes, but the
basic affinity with his natural hand shows through on every page. The poems
appear to have been carefully written out at different times into notebooks,
each being torn out on completion and sent separately to the actress (two
different makes of paper are represented among the manuscripts).

These eighteen love poems have been the subject of con-
siderable controversy in recent years. Discovered in the early
1950s by the London antiquarian bookseller, Mr Peter Eaton,
the original manuscripts were accepted as genuine Shaw and
sold as such by Sotheby's on 22 April 1958. Later, doubts were
cast in certain quarters on their authenticity, and Sotheby's
withdrew their certification of the poems, and some authorities
on Shaw deny that they are his work. The entry in Sotheby's

[5]

Violet Beverley

No matter how cleverly
I try to work when you sit beside me
At set of sun
There is nothing done
Only the unwritten page to chide me
Only your empty chair to deride me

It is something to have learned your name
And something more to have heard your voice
Though I came not hither with any such aim
Though you sat beside me by chance, not choice.
Oh Violet, Violet, why do you come
To read about your primeval kind
To a place where men must be deaf and dumb
But where, alas! they must not be blind?
I came to write, and I stayed to look
I dared not offend, yet could not refrain
And so, whilst you sat there deep in your book
I studied your face again and again.

And thus, Miss Beverly
No matter how cleverly
I strive to work as you sit beside me
At set of sun
I have nothing done

There is only my?/unwritten page to chide me
Only your empty chair to divide me.

11th April 1882

Subsequently there is reason to believe that her name, after
all, is not Violet Beverly, but Mabel Crofton Consequently —

Mabel Crofton
No matter how often
I turn to my work when you et de ac

and — Oh Mabel Crofton why do you come
or — Oh moidering Mabel, why

catalogue reproduced the manuscript of one of the poems (see
the facsimile of the catalogue entry on page 5, reproduced by
permission of Sotheby's).

It is indeed true that the handwriting of the poems is not
absolutely identical with Shaw's normal calligraphy; but there
are numerous striking similarities, as the reader may confirm
from the facsimile on pages 6/7 of an acknowledged authentic
specimen of his handwriting, a typically witty love poem entitled
'Violet Beverly', reproduced by permission of The Society of
Authors on behalf of the Bernard Shaw Estate. It is of course
possible that the variations in the writing could have been a

deliberate attempt at disguise on Shaw's part, and it is not a far stretch of the imagination to wonder whether he might have intended to send the poems to Ellen Terry under a somewhat transparent cloak of anonymity. Shaw delighted in such playful pranks throughout his life. Other more mundane explanations could be put forward. Certainly for my own part I see no valid reason to doubt the authenticity of the manuscripts, and remain convinced that the poems are genuine Shaw. No one will find it easy to deny that their charm, their sentiments, and much of their phrasing are Shavian.

The late Miss Blanche Patch, Shaw's last private secretary, told me shortly before her death some years ago that H. G. Wells had once remarked to Shaw after seeing one of his plays that he (Shaw) could not control his wit and love of larking, urging him to 'dull himself with meat' and then he would be a great dramatist: a gratuitous piece of advice which Shaw, a strict vegetarian all his life, no doubt duly appreciated.

As Shaw proved in these and other serious verses, he *could* indeed 'control his wit', if not also his 'love of larking'. Another intriguing anecdote from Miss Patch's rich store deals somewhat more pathetically with the same subject:

> I remember hearing G.B.S. telling some students at the Royal Academy of Dramatic Art that he sometimes felt he had achieved the heights of literary fame and said to himself: 'I am there; I am at the top. And then Joey the Clown pops out between my legs and I can never resist him . . .'

These eighteen beautiful love poems for the equally beautiful Ellen Terry demonstrate, however, how well Shaw could—and did—resist 'Joey the Clown'.

The nineteen enchanting photographs of the celebrated actress at various stages in her theatrical career which adorn this collection will be found a fitting complement to her admirer's eloquent tribute.

JACK WERNER

[8]

George Bernard Shaw

Born in Dublin on 26 July, 1856, George Bernard Shaw (he intensely disliked his first name George, which he made a practice of ignoring) attended various schools in that city, leaving at the age of 15½, and later declared that he had learned absolutely nothing at any of them. At home and at the National Gallery of Ireland, however, he acquired a considerable degree of culture in operatic and religious music as well as in literature and painting. He continued his self-education at the British Museum after he left Dublin at the age of 20 for London, where his mother had already established herself as a teacher of singing. Thanks to the influence of friends, he became successively a music, art and dramatic critic on *The Star*, (as 'Corno di Bassetto'), *The World* and *The Saturday Review* respectively, and in each of these fields he expressed the most decided, dogmatic and provocative opinions.

Shaw became an ardent Socialist and helped to build up the Socialist party in England. In 1884 he joined the Fabian Society, and as an open-air speaker he proved more than a match for his opponents by his wit, repartee and clarity of argument.

From 1879-83 Shaw wrote a number of novels, all of which failed to find a publisher. He then turned to the sphere of drama, writing one play after another with remarkable rapidity, each play being accompanied by a challenging Preface in some cases equalling the play in length, and very soon established himself as the greatest dramatist since Shakespeare. His total output of plays exceeds fifty.

Shaw was offered a peerage and the Order of Merit when Labour first came to power in 1924. He characteristically refused both, saying he did not wish to sit in the House of Lords,

(*above*) 'Shaw's Corner' at Ayot St Lawrence with his last private
secretary, Miss Blanche Patch; an unpublished snapshot taken by Shaw

(*right*) GBS at the rehearsal of *Arms and the Man* at the Avenue Theatre,
London, on 21 April 1894; from the drawing by Sir Bernard Partridge
(*Mansell Collection*)

Ahenobarbus
at Rehsarsal.

An unpublished snapshot of GBS taken by Miss Blanche Patch on the balcony of his flat at Whitehall Court

and that he had already conferred the OM upon himself. The following year, however, he was awarded and accepted the Nobel prize for literature. He married in 1898 a wealthy Irish woman, Miss Charlotte Payne-Townshend (to whom he occasionally and somewhat flippantly referred as 'my Irish millionairess').

Throughout his life Shaw was a rigid vegetarian, and from his youth was greatly interested in boxing. From 1906 until his death on 2 November 1950, at the age of 94, he lived in the village of Ayot St Lawrence, Herts, naming his house 'Shaw's Corner'.

Ellen Terry

Dame Ellen Alicia Terry was born in Coventry, Warwickshire, on 27 February, 1847, the daughter of an actor, Benjamin Terry. She made her first stage appearance, at the age of 9, as the boy Mamillius in Shakespeare's *The Winter's Tale* at the Princess's Theatre, followed by Puck in *A Midsummer Night's Dream*, and Arthur in *King John*. They were the first of numerous stage-roles, and she became one of the greatest actresses in the history of the British theatre, adulated in both Britain and the USA. Her interpretation of Portia in *The Merchant of Venice* was celebrated throughout the English-speaking world and has never been surpassed. Her exquisite voice and subtle use of gesture were particularly notable in her Shakespearian performances.

Ellen Terry was Shaw's favourite actress. He was fascinated by her beauty and qualities of mind, to which he paid eloquent tribute in their celebrated 'paper courtship' from the mid-1890s. She had written to *The Star* to ask advice on behalf of a young friend interested in becoming an opera star. Shaw replied, though their real corrrespondence started three years later in 1895. He was vehemently critical of the English theatre, considering that it was old-fashioned and thus wasteful of many new talents. His prime object of attack was the noted actor-manager, Sir Henry Irving of the Lyceum Theatre. For 30 years Ellen Terry had served Irving faithfully as leading lady in numerous Shakespearean plays. Shaw was convinced that her gifts could be more fruitfully used in the modern theatre, and wrote frequently to her of the Norwegian dramatist Ibsen. Later he wrote *Captain Brassbound's Conversion* for her, but she turned the part down. She was, however, eventually persuaded to star in it in 1905. He

Ellen Terry as Beatrice in *Much Ado About Nothing*

Ellen Terry's last home, 'Smallhythe Place' in Kent, now administered by The National Trust as an Ellen Terry Memorial (*The National Trust*)

never wrote another part specially for her, though she did play the leading role in a number of his plays. Their relationship had one strange aspect—they refused to meet until 1900, when some quality in their attitude towards each other appeared to have been lost.

Ellen Terry married three times, but she continued to regard Shaw as one of her closest friends. Her first marriage was in 1866, to the celebrated painter George Frederick Watts, whose model she had been and who was thirty years her senior. The marriage lasted barely nine months. Her second, in 1877, was to an actor, Charles Kelly, and finally, in 1907, to an American actor, James

[15]

The Terry Room at 'Smallhythe Place' (*The National Trust*)

Carew, who was this time thirty years her junior. Her last appearance on the stage was in 1925, and she later appeared in films and in Shakespearian lecture-recitals both in Britain and the USA. She died on 21 July, 1928, at her cottage, 'Smallhythe Place' in Kent, which became an Ellen Terry Memorial Museum and in 1939 was presented to the National Trust by her daughter, Edith Craig.

Ellen Terry's elder sister Kate, an actress of considerable reputation, had a daughter, also Kate, who became the mother of Val Gielgud and Sir John Gielgud.

The Love Poems

Ellen Terry in 1856 at the age of seven

1

Lady, wilt thou love me?
  Prithee, say me aye!
By Heaven that's above me,
  I die if thou say nay!
Life is naught without thee
  Gloomy is the day: —
Lady, wilt thou love me?
  Prithee, say me aye.

Ellen Terry in 1856 at the age of seven

Ellen Terry in 1864 at the age of sixteen

2

O I know not why I love thee!
  'Tis not that thou art so fair;
Tho' the sun that shines above thee
  Be no brighter than thy hair,
Were thy locks as black as hell,
I should love thee just as well.

'Tis not that thine eyes are blue
  Like the flowers in the corn;
Were they of another hue,
  All unlike them I should scorn;
Were they greener than the sea,
'Twould not change my love for thee.

Neither is it that thy kindness
  Won that heart; my hapless lot
Is to love in utter blindness
  One, alas! who knows it not.
One whose touch I shall not feel,
At whose feet I may not kneel.

Unrequited tho' it be,
  Tho' I know not whence it came,
Still, the love I bear to thee
  Dies must remain the same;
Ceasing then alone to live,
When I have no heart to give.

Ellen Terry at the age of seventeen after her first marriage to the painter, George Frederick Watts, in 1864; a photograph by the celebrated Victorian photographer Mrs Julia Margaret Cameron

3

If there be aught beneath the skies
Whose vision I most dearly prize,—
  Sweetest Lady, 'tis thine eyes.

If there be aught on earth that's fair,
For which most tenderly I care,—
  Sweetest Lady, 'tis thy hair.

If aught doth my poor heart beguile,
Of which I dream the day's whole while,
  Sweetest Lady, 'tis thy smile.

Ellen Terry in 1874 as Philippa in *The Wandering Heir* by Charles Reade

4

O! I could watch Her face all day
And never turn mine eyes away:
   On earth She has no peer.
I wonder who — once knowing Her, —
Can dare another to prefer.

O! I could silent lie all day
If She one word to me would say:
   When Her sweet voice I hear,
I wonder how the birds can sing
And not be mute for listening.

O! I should never stir all day
If She Her hand in mine would lay:
   To me She is so dear,
I wonder how to know true bliss
Till I have felt my Lady's kiss.

Kate Terry, Ellen's elder sister, sitting at a mirror, though the reflection is that of Ellen Terry

5

Time, heavy Time, O lift thy leaden wings,
Turn weeks to days, and weary days to hours!
When She is far, in vain the skylark sings;
Scentless and faded are the sickening flowers.

Fly then, O Time! Bring joy to me apace!
When She is near, all pain and sorrow dies;
To stand where I might always see Her face,
Would make of Hell itself a Paradise!

Ellen Terry and Mrs Stirling (later Lady Gregory) as Juliet and
her Nurse in *Romeo and Juliet*

6

Days have passed, and months, and years,
Since I found that Love was Sorrow:
  Of what avail are sighs and tears
  If they bring no joy the morrow?
    Ah! this world is full of pain,
    I've prayed for Love, but all in vain.

Days will pass, and months, and years,
Love, to me, shall still be Sorrow:
  Hush, fond sighs! — and tarry, tears!
  Joy will never come the morrow.
    Ah! this world is full of pain.
    I've prayed for Love, but all in vain.

Ellen Terry in 1886

7

I weep because the light is gone,
  Because today is dead:
Because too soon the fickle skies,
  With sad hue now o'erspread,
  Will don a garb of garish red
To greet an unknown morn:
  Because another sun must rise,
A new today be born.

I weep because today was blest.
  Because today was dear:
Because too many hours shall roll
  Ere thou again be near;
  Because lip, palm, and eye, and ear
Strain after thee in futile quest:
  Because I want thee from my soul,
And, wanting, find no rest.

Ellen Terry in *The Belle's Stratagem* by Mrs Hannah Cowley

8

When Love first set this little lute
In my unskilful hand,
'Twas Sorrow taught me how to sweep
The strings in unison, and weep
My woes to one poor tune. Fain now
To strike new chords, I know not how;
And, finding that I understand
No merry tones, sit mute.

For sweet Content hath passed this way
And —smiling at my woes—
Drawn me her flower'd path along,
Filling my heart with a glad new song.
But O how can I sing of bliss,
To such a sorry chord as this?
I'll wait I hope for that fair day
When Love shall teach me all he knows.

Sir Henry Irving and Ellen Terry as the Vicar and Olivia in a dramatised version by W. G. Wills of Goldsmith's *Vicar of Wakefield*

9

Lady moon, that sailest high
In the bleak and dreary sky,
From thy lonely post above,
Tell me, dost thou see my Love?

Many a time, O moon, at night
Thou hast cheered Her with thy light;
How I envy thee thy lot!
I, alas, can serve Her not.

When in bed She lies asleep,
Thro' the window thou canst peep,
On Her beauty freely gaze
And kiss Her eyelids with thy rays.

I, alas, must tarry here,
Never see my Lady dear,
Never e'en Her fingers kiss.
O! 'tis sad to love like this!

Ellen Terry as Portia in *The Merchant of Venice*

10

Hark! the winter wind doth wail,
  And the winter night is drear:
Tho' the moon shines, silver pale,
  Tho' the twinkling stars be clear,
There has risen a misty veil,
Hiding all their light from here.

And my Love, who is my light,
  Only shines for other eyes:
Fate, to hide His from my sight,
  Like a cloud doth ever rise,
Till my heart's more black than night,
Drearier than the lightless skies.

Ellen Terry as Ophelia in *Hamlet*

11

Goodnight, beloved. The year is on the wane,
Its joys have passed, together with its pain;
Or good or bad, 'twill not return again.

Out of the ashes of the year that dies,
Another, Phoenix-like—must now arise:
O be it glad and joyful in thine eyes!

May'st thou lack nought that to thy heart is dear
Be sorrow far from thee, and comfort near,
Thro' all the changes of the coming year.

Sleep soft — wake gladly with the dawn of day!
Goodnight, beloved. The year has passed away.

Ellen Terry in 1888

12

Sweet Lady, if the sun were mine
  And willing to obey,
For thy dear sake I'd bid him shine
  Unceasingly this day;
No cloud should pass, no mist arise
To hide his radiance from thine eyes.

If, at my bidding, trees could bear
  And dry stems burst to bloom,
The earth should teem with flowers fair,
  Dispelling winter's gloom:
Each spot where thou didst set thy feet
Should bring forth blossoms, fresh and sweet

For, since there dwelleth none on earth
  I love so well as thee,
The blessed day that gave thee birth
  Is the day of days for me.
And nature's voice I long to raise,
Too weak alone to sing thy praise.

Ellen Terry as Imogen in *Cymbeline*

13

God made thee in a lavish mood,
      O Mistress mine!
Nothing sweet or true or fine
Was stinted in thy spirit's make:
Transcendent beauty He did take
      And render thine,
Endowing thee with perfect womanhood.

      O Mistress mine!
Since so much hast thou more than we,
What wonder is it if to thee
      More pain was given?
If, having all too large a share
Of God's good, He — the Ever-Fair —
Scourged thee to prove the justice of His Heaven?

Ellen Terry as Catherine Duval in *The Dead Heart* in 1889, a melodrama described by Ellen Terry as 'small beer'

14

Light of my heart! . Behold, with trembling hand
  These sorry leaves upon thy path I strew:
  In no wise worthy, saving that they grew
On the green branches of a deathless tree,
Planted —long since— within my breast by thee.

Stoop not to heed them! On the shifting sand
  Of time, thy footsteps will be deep and clear.
  I only ask thee to walk·on, that here
My love may linger, when all else is dead,
Within the hallow'd trace of thy foot's tread.

Ellen Terry in her study at 'Smallhythe Place'

6. Thou Eternal Spirit, who art One
With all that is,—God! whose unmeasur'd sway
Doth compass all, whose law the stars obey,
The watchfull moon, and glory-shedding sun:-
Maker of earth, who bade the waters run
Into the toiling sea, Thy voice can stay
The ocean's wrath,—behold! I crouch and pray!
Stretch forth Thy hand! Bid that Thy will be done!—

Frail is the vessel, toss'd by surf and foam
On the black bosom of engulfing death—
At Thy command the rival waves will part,
The warring winds, with sweet harmonious breath
Waft Her into the haven of Her home,
And lull the fear that watcheth in my heart.

Ellen Terry as Hermione in *The Winter's Tale*

16

Lady my love, this foolish heart of mine,
Choked with poor fragments of unutter'd song,
Searches in vain, amidst a tangled throng
Of lifeless sonnets, for one breathing line
In which to speak the love that still is thine.
O happy heart! whose faith—enduring long—
Has hushed the voice that taxed it once with wrong.
O happy eyes! that revel in the shine
Of the same sun that glorified their youth,
That—child and woman—shed the same sweet tears!
Yet, I have heard it said that love is frail,
With no more strength to face the storms of years
Than blossoms, scattered in a single gale.
Those only who have loved can know the truth.

A portrait of Ellen Terry

17

O wind of Heaven, that whistles in the eaves,
Spirit! what is thy will?
I watch thee toss the quaking leaves
And dance athwart the corn,
And thou art never still:
Whirling, wailing, night and morn,
Dusk and day;
Thy fell path strewn with flowers uptorn
Upon thy way.

O wind of Heaven, that whispers in mine ear
Spirit! what wouldst thou tell?
Breath of the West thou bearest here,
Monarch of mighty wing!
And there She now doth dwell:
Knowst thou, Her voice's echo bearing
East from West,
No comfort to me bring?
O wind of Heaven, save me from despairing,
Or be at rest.

A charming vignette of Ellen Terry

18

Now I bethink me of it, Lady sweet,
It is no wonder if thou art so kind,
For thou indeed hast little right to mind
This load of love, new laid beneath thy feet.
Unwittingly, thyself hast made it meet
That thus it be. Midst thy bright locks entwin'd,
Right-giving reasons without end I find;
Stringent commands to love thee have a seat
Upon thy chin, the lashes of thine eyes;
Whilst thy lips' music, dancing in each ear,
Loud bids me hold thee evermore most dear.
I ask thee then, how should thy choler rise
At finding that I boldly love thee less,
Since 'tis obedient to thine own behest?

1

Lady, wilt thou love me?
 Prithee, say me aye!
By Heaven that's above me,
 I die if thou say nay!
Life is naught without thee,
 Gloomy is the day:—
Lady, wilt thou love me?
 Prithee, say me aye.

2

O I know not why I love thee!
 'Tis not that thou art so fair;
Tho' the sun that shines above thee
 Be no brighter than thy hair,
Were thy locks as black as hell,
I should love thee just as well.

'Tis not that thine eyes are blue
 Like the flowers in the corn;
Were they of another hue,
 All unlike them I should scorn.
Were they greener than the sea,
'Twould not change my love for thee.

Neither is it that thy kindness
 Won this heart; my hapless lot
Is to love in utter blindness
 One, alas! who knows it not.
One whose touch I shall not feel,
At whose feet I may not kneel.

Unrequited tho' it be,
   Tho' I know not whence it came,
Still, the love I bear to thee
   Ever must remain the same ;
Ceasing then alone to live,
When I have no heart to give.

3

If there be aught beneath the skies
Whose vision I most dearly prize,—
   Sweetest Lady, 'tis thine eyes.

If there be aught on earth that's fair,
For which most tenderly I care—
   Sweetest Lady, 'tis thy hair.

If aught doth my poor heart beguile,
Of which I dream the day's whole while,—
   Sweetest Lady, 'tis thy smile.

4

O ! I could watch Her face all day
And never turn mine eyes away:
On earth She has no peer.
I wonder who—once knowing Her,—
Can dare another to prefer.

O! I could silent lie all day
If She one word to me would say:
When Her sweet voice I hear,
I wonder how the birds can sing
And not be mute for listening.

O! I should never stir all day
If She Her hand in mine would lay:
   To me She is so dear,
I wonder how to know true bliss
Till I have felt my Lady's kiss.

5

Time, heavy Time, O lift thy leaden wings,
Turn weeks to days, and weary days to hours!
When She is far, in vain the skylark sings;
Scentless and faded are the sick'ning flowers.

Fly then, O Time! Bring joy to me apace!
When She is near, all pain and sorrow dies;
To stand where I might always see Her face,
Would make of Hell itself a Paradise!

6

Days have passed, and months, and years,
Since I found that Love was Sorrow:
   Of what avail are sighs and tears
If they bring no joy the morrow?
     Ah! this world is full of pain,
     I've prayed for Love, but all in vain.

Days will pass, and months, and years,
Love, to me, shall still be Sorrow:
　　Hush, fond sighs!—and tarry, tears!
Joy will never come the morrow.
　　　　Ah! this world is full of pain,
　　　　I've prayed for Love, but all in vain.

7

I weep because the light is gone,
　　Because today is dead:
Because too soon the fickle skies,
　　With sad hue now o'erspread,
　　Will don a garb of garish red
To greet an unknown morn:
　　Because another sun must rise,
A new today be born.

I weep because today was blest,
　　Because today was dear:
Because too many hours shall roll
　　Ere thou again be near:
　　Because lip, palm, and eye, and ear
Strain after thee in futile quest:
　　Because I want thee from my soul,
And, wanting, find no rest.

8

When Love first set this little lute
In my unskilful hand,
'Twas Sorrow taught me how to sweep
The strings in unison, and weep
My woes to one poor tune. Fain now
To strike new chords, I know not how;
And, finding that I understand
No merry tones, sit mute.

For sweet Content hath passed this way
And—smiling at my woes—
Drawn me her flower'd path along,
Filling my heart with a glad new song.
But O how can I sing of bliss
To such a sorry chord as this?
I'll wait and hope for that fair day
When Love shall teach me all he knows.

9

Lady moon, that sailest high
In the bleak and dreary sky,
From thy lonely post above,
Tell me, dost thou see my Love?

Many a time, O moon, at night
Thou hast cheered Her with thy light:
How I envy thee thy lot!
I, alas, can serve Her not.

When in bed She lies asleep,
Thro' the window thou canst peep,
On Her beauty freely gaze
And kiss Her eyelids with thy rays.

I, alas, must tarry here,
Never see my Lady dear,
Never e'en Her fingers kiss.
O! 'tis sad to love like this!

10

Hark! the winter wind doth wail,
   And the winter night is drear:
Tho' the moon shines, silver pale,
   Tho' the twinkling stars be clear,
There has risen a misty veil,
Hiding all their light from here.

And my Love, who is my light,
   Only shines for other eyes:
Fate, to hide Her from my sight,
   Like a cloud doth ever rise,
Till my heart's more black than night,
Drearier than the lightless skies.

11

Goodnight, beloved. The year is on the wane,
Its joys have passed, together with its pain;
Or good or bad, 'twill not return again.

Out of the ashes of the year that dies,
Another, Phoenix-like, must now arise;
O be it glad and joyful in thine eyes!

May'st thou lack nought that to thy heart is dear;
Be sorrow far from thee, and comfort near,
Thro' all the changes of the coming year.

Sleep soft—wake gladly with the dawn of day!
Goodnight, beloved. The year has passed away.

12

Sweet Lady, if the sun were mine
   And willing to obey,
For thy dear sake I'd bid him shine
   Unceasingly this day:
No cloud should pass, no mist arise
To hide his radiance from thine eyes.

If, at my bidding, trees could bear
   And dry stems burst to bloom,
The earth should teem with flowers fair,
   Dispelling winter's gloom:
Each spot where thou did'st set thy feet
Should bring forth blossoms, fresh and sweet.

For, since there dwelleth none on earth
   I love so well as thee,
The blessed day that gave thee birth
   Is the day of days for me.
And nature's voice I long to raise,
Too weak alone to sing thy praise.

13

God made thee in a lavish mood,
    O Mistress mine!
Nothing sweet or true or fine
Was stinted in thy spirit's make:
Transcendent beauty He did take
    And render thine,
Endowing thee with perfect womanhood.

    O Mistress mine!
Since so much hast thou more than we,
What wonder is it if to thee
    More pain was given?
If, having all too large a share
Of God's good, He—the Ever-fair—
Scourged thee to prove the justice of His Heaven?

14

Light of my heart! Behold, with trembling hand
    These sorry leaves upon thy path I strew:
    In no wise worthy, saving that they grew
On the green branches of a deathless tree,
Planted—long since—within my breast by thee.

Stoop not to heed them! On the shifting sand
    Of time, thy footsteps will be deep and clear.
    I only ask thee to walk on, that here
My love may linger, when all else is dead,
Within the hallowed trace of thy foot's tread.

15

O! Thou Eternal Spirit, who art One
With all that is—God! whose unmeasur'd sway
Doth compass all, whose law the stars obey,
The watchful moon, and glory-shedding sun!
Maker of earth, who bade the waters run
Into the toiling sea, Thy voice can stay
The ocean's wrath, behold! I crouch and pray!
Stretch forth Thy hand! Bid that Thy will be done!
Frail is the vessel, toss'd by surf and foam
On the black bosom of engulfing death—
At Thy command the rival waves will part,
The warring winds, with sweet harmonious breath
Waft Her into the haven of Her home,
And lull the fear that watcheth in my heart.

16

Lady my Love, this foolish heart of mine,
Choked with poor fragments of unutter'd song,
Searches in vain, amidst a tangled throng
Of lifeless sonnets, for one breathing line
In which to speak the Love that still is thine.
O, happy heart! whose faith—enduring long—
Has hushed the voice that taxed it once with wrong.
O, happy eyes! that revel in the shine
Of the same sun that glorified their youth,
That—child and woman—shed the same sweet tears!
Yet, I have heard it said that Love is frail,
With no more strength to face the storms of years
Than blossoms, scattered in a single gale.
Those only who have loved can know the truth.

17

O wind of Heaven, that whistles in the eaves,
Spirit! what is thy will?
I watch thee toss the quaking leaves
And dance athwart the corn;
And thou art never still:
Whirling, wailing, night and morn,
Dusk and day:
Thy fell path strewn with flowers uptorn
Upon thy way.

O wind of Heaven, that whispers in mine ear,
Spirit! what wouldst thou tell?
Breath of the West thou bearest here,
Monarch of mighty wing!
And there She now doth dwell:
Canst thou, Her voice's echo bearing
East from West,
No comfort to me bring?
O wind of Heaven, save me from despairing!
Or be at rest.

18

Now I bethink me of it, Lady sweet,
It is no wonder if thou art so kind,
For thou indeed hast little right to mind
This load of love, new laid beneath thy feet.
Unwittingly, thyself hast made it meet [*sic*]
That thus it be. Midst thy bright locks entwin'd,
Right-giving reasons without end I find;
Stringent commands to love thee have a seat
Upon thy chin, the lashes of thine eyes;
Whilst thy lips' music, dancing in each ear,
Loud bids me hold thee evermore most dear.
I ask thee, then, how should thy choler rise
At finding that I boldly love thee best,
Since 'tis obedient to thine own behest?

NB All spelling and punctuation is typeset exactly as in the original manuscripts